A Kalmus Classic Edition

Alexander
GRETCHANINOFF

FIVE LITTLE PIECES

Opus 3

FOR PIANO

K 02139

CONTENTS

Plainte.....**5**

Meditation.....**8**

Chant d' automne.....**11**

Orage.....**13**

Nocturne.....**17**

ALEXANDER GRETCHANINOFF
(1864-1956)

Russian composer, Alexander Gretchaninoff was born in Moscow where he began his study of piano at the age of 14. He left school at 17 to go to Moscow Conservatory where he studied with such notables as Arensky, Gubert, Kashkin, Larosh and Safonoff. Here he studied piano, counterpoint and theory, and soon became familiar with operas, orchestral and chamber music. In 1893 he left the Moscow Conservatory and moved his studies to the St. Petersburg Conservatory with Rimsky-Korsakov. Soon after this his compositions began to win acclaim and performance. Rimsky-Korsakov even conducted Gretchaninoff's First Symphony.

Gretchaninoff taught piano in St. Petersburg and Moscow, and became very involved with Moscow University, the Berkman Music School and the Gnesin Institute, where he taught. He made an attempt at composing opera, but had only one success. He was better known for his piano and orchestral compositions as well as a number of songs. It is said he was highly influenced by the music of Tchaikowsky, Borodin and Rimsky-Korsakov.

Following the Revolution, Gretchaninoff left his home country and traveled through Europe, finally settling for a while in Paris where he continued to compose and perform as a pianist. In 1929 he made his first of several visits to America, and made New York his permanent home in 1930.

FIVE LITTLE PIECES

I. Plainte

Alexander Gretchaninoff

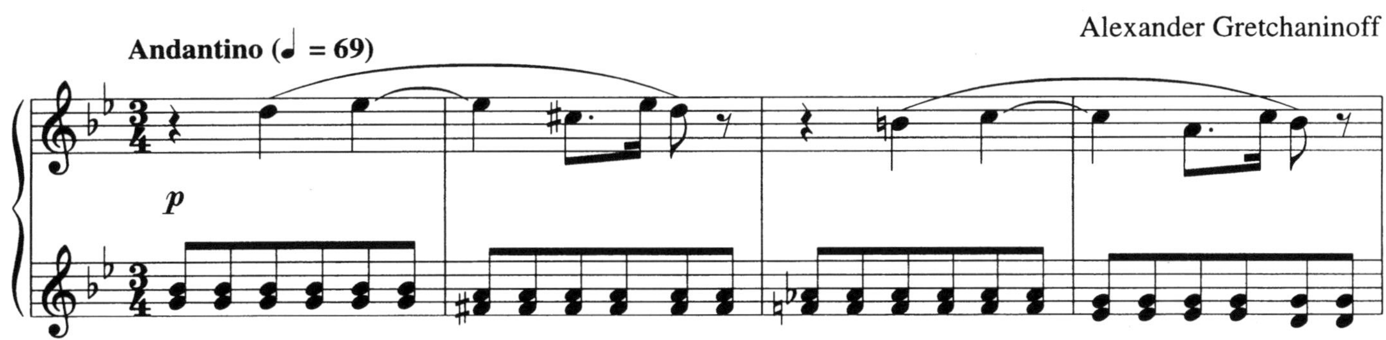

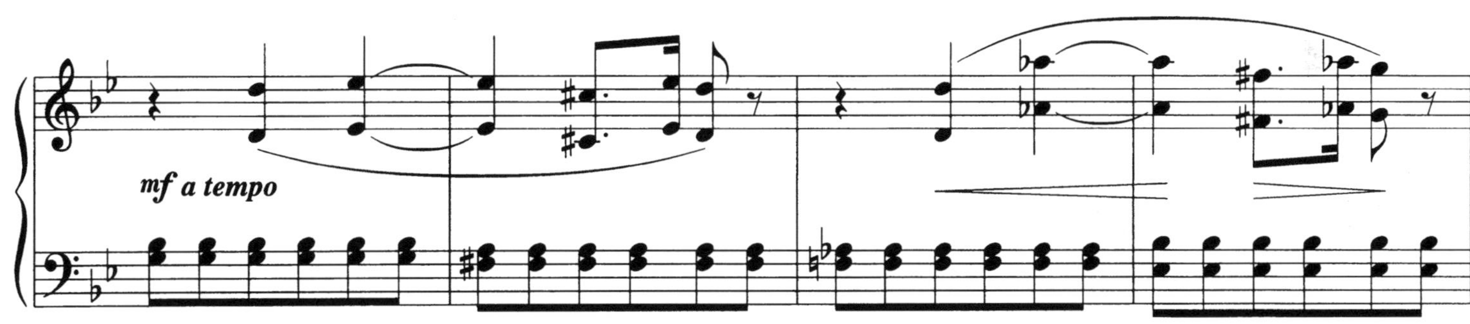

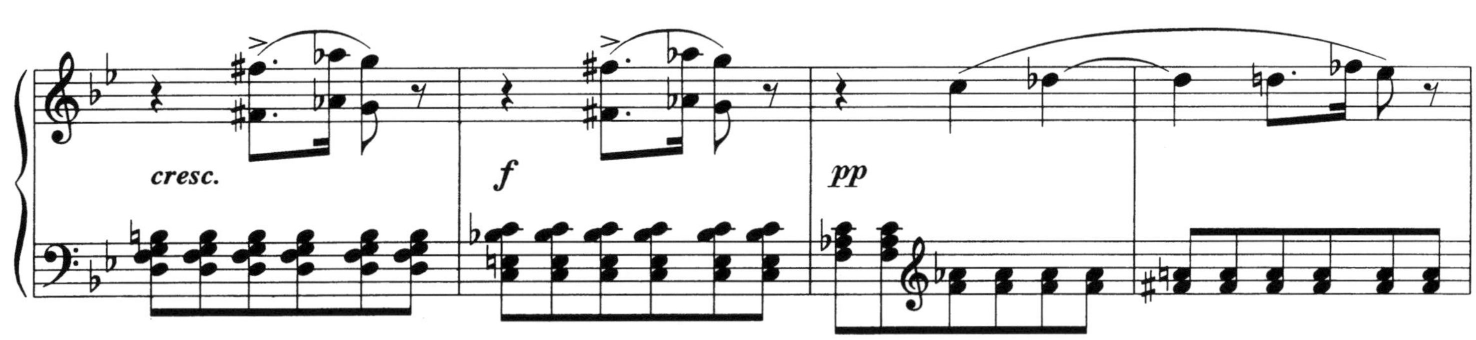

poco string
rit.
p a tempo
rit. e dim.
a tempo
ff
rubato
più f disperatione

dim.
p
pp morendo
ppp

II. Méditation

Allegretto (♩ = 126)
pp
mf
f
3
p
3
3
3
3

L'istesso tempo
p
pp leggiero
l.h.
f
pp
mf
sf

III. Chant d'Automne

f p
mf
Tempo I
p
f
3 3 3
3 3 3
p
5
5
5
5
5 1 2
3 3 3 3 3 3
pp
pp

IV. Orage

Vivo (♩ = 120)
p
8va
accel.
sf
mf
sf
a tempo p
accel. molto
8va
sf
f
a tempo

r.h.
più f
sff ff
Più mosso
p doloroso
sff
ff
p
sff
ff
p
8va
sff
mf
molto cresc.
8va
trem.

8va
sff
mf
molto cresc.
(8va)
8va
p
cresc.
(8va)
ff
(8va)
mf più tranquillo

8va
p
quasitrem.
p
8va
p
8va
p
(8va)
Più lento
poco rit.
morendo
ppp

V. Nocturne

accel. poco a poco e cresc.
rit.
p più tranquillo
pp
lento
8va
Poco più mosso, ma sempre tranq. (♩. = 76)
mf
f
mf

Tempo I
lento
espress.
p
p
p
Più lento
p
pp
ad lib.
rit.
f
molto rit.
morendo
ppp
rit.